It's Laugh O'Clock

O'Clock

Joke Book

Easter Edition

With Fun Illustrations

Hundreds of Jokes That Kids and Family Will Enjoy

RIDDLELAND

Design elements from Freepik.com

Table of Contents

Riddleland Bonus Book

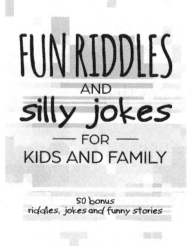

http://pixelfy.me/riddlelandbonus

Thank you for buying this book. We would like to share a special bonus as a token of appreciation. It is a collection of 50 original jokes, riddles, and two super funny stories!

Join our **Facebook Group** at **Riddleland for Kids** to get daily jokes and riddles.

Introduction

"There are always flowers for those who want to see them." ~ **Henri Matisse**

Get ready to laugh! *It's Laugh O'Clock Joke Book: Easter Edition* is different from other joke books. This book is not meant to be read alone - although it can be; instead it is a game to be played with siblings, friends, family or between two people to see who can make the other laugh first. It's time to laugh; it's always laugh o'clock somewhere.

These jokes are written to provide a fun, quality reading experience. Children learn best when they are playing; reading is fun when it is something one wants to read, and most children want to read jokes. Reading jokes will increase vocabulary and comprehension. Jokes also have many other benefits:

- **Bonding** – Sharing this book is an excellent way for parents and children to spend some quality time having fun, sharing laughs, and making memories.

- **Building Confidence** - When parents ask one of the jokes, it creates a safe environment for children to burst out answers even if they are incorrect.
  This helps children to develop self-confidence and self-expression.

- **Improve Vocabulary** – Jokes are a lot of fun, and that makes reading a lot of fun. Children will need to understand the words if they want to understand the jokes.

- **Enhancing Reading Comprehension** – Many children can read at a young age but may not understand the context of words in the sentences. Jokes, especially puns, can help develop children's interest to comprehend the context.

- **Developing Creativity** – Funny, creative jokes can help children develop their sense of humor while getting their brains working. Many times a word in a joke can be taken two ways, and picturing it both ways leads to creative imagery.

- **Developing Logical Thinking Skills** – Because many jokes have a dual play on words, children must use logic to decide which meaning the speaker intended.

 Enjoy the book, and, remember, it's always laugh o'clock somewhere.

Rules of the Game

The goal is to make your opponent laugh

- Face your opponent
  Stare at them!

- Make funny faces and noises to
  throw your opponent off

- Take turns reading the jokes out
  loud to each other

- When someone laughs, the other
  person wins a point

First person to get 5 points,
is crowned the Champion!

FUN FACTS FOR EASTER

Do you know which country made the first Easter Egg?

It was the UK, and it was made in a place called Bristol, in 1873, by a chocolate company called Fry's.

Do you know where the largest Easter egg hunt took place?

It was in 2007, in Florida. There were over 501,000 eggs that were hunted by 9,753 children.

CHAPTER 1

The Easter Egg Q&A Challenge

Did you know the tradition of giving Easter eggs originated from Medieval Europe? The egg is a symbol of new life, fertility, and rebirth in many cultures.

What is the favorite dance of the Easter Bunny?

It is called the bunny hop!

Why was the Easter Bunny mad after leaving the barber shop?

He had a bad hare-cut, and they wouldn't give him a refund!

How do you know that carrots are good for your eyes?

You never see rabbits wearing any glasses!

What is the favorite sport of Easter Bunnies?

They love basket-ball since they are so good at stuffing baskets!

After discussing the possibility of going around the world on Easter eve, why did the Easter Bunny only take even numbered eggs?

He was told the odds weren't good.

What is always at the end of Easter?

'R.'

How do you catch the Easter Bunny?

You should hide behind a tree and make carrot noises.

Why does the Easter bunny love carrots?

Because he wants to have great eyesight.

How do you make Easter Bunny stew?

You make him wait for a long time!

What songs do teenage Easter Bunnies listen to in a car?

They listen to hip hop songs!

What kind of jewelry does the Spring bunny wear?

She wears the latest 14-carrot gold rings!

Where did the doctor Easter Bunny attend school?

He went to John Hop-kins University!

What food do rabbits use as a hot tub?

Soup; many people have reported to waiters seeing hares in the soup.

Why did the Easter bunny hide behind the sofa?

It is because he was a little chicken.

What is the Easter Bunny's favorite vegetable?

Eggplants cooked any way.

What did the doctor advise the hen to do?

Lay off eggs for a week.

Why do chickens lay eggs?

If the chickens dropped the eggs, they would break!

How are spring flowers and the letter "A" similar?

It is because a 'bee' comes after them both.

Why did the Easter Bunny feel so foolish when he noticed food on his whiskers?

It had been under his nose the whole time.

Why is the Easter Bunny the luckiest animal in the world?

He has four rabbit's feet!

What happened when the Easter Bunny met his wife?

They got married and lived hopp-ily ever after!

Which Easter bunnies can never hop no matter how hard they try?

The chocolate covered ones!

When you mix a bunny and a bee together, what do you get?

You get a honey bunny!

What is the fastest way to send a letter to the Easter Bunny?

You should use the hare-mail service.

Where can you find the most Easter eggs after Easter?

The clearance racks!

What is the favorite story of the Easter Bunny?

Any story that has a hoppy ending!

What do you get when you make the Easter Bunny stand outside on the sidewalk on a hot day?

You get a hot cross bunny!

What happened when the egg ran into the school?

It made a real mess.

Why did the baby egg keep getting in trouble?

He kept egg-aggerating his stories!

What is the Easter egg's favorite activity?

It is rolling cross country!

What do people sing to the Easter Bunny on his birthday?

Hoppy Birthday!

Have you ever tried to hunt Easter eggs blindfolded?

You don't know what you're missing.

What should you do if you have an Easter egg infestation?

Call the eggs- terminator!

Why did the hen watch the mason worker in amazement?

She heard he was going to lay a brick.

Why couldn't the eggs ever watch their favorite television show on TV?

Their signal was scrambled.

What is the name of the egg that's always pulling pranks?

The practical yolker.

Have you seen the Easter Bunny at the mall; how did he look?

When I saw him, he looked with his eyes.

What did the girl say when she found an Easter egg stuffed in the couch?

"Sofa, so good."

What is the Easter Bunny's favorite breakfast food?

A honey bun!

How would you update the old adage for Easter: If you can't beat them?	What happened when the Easter Bunny's egg coloring team quit?
Hard boil them.	He had dyer needs.

What kind of shoes does the Easter Bunny wear to walk quietly?

Sneakers.

What did the grouch say when he saw the Easter Bunny start putting eggs on his lawn?

"Hare we go again."

What is the world's most famous Easter Bunny military General?

Napoleon Bunnyparte!

What does the hair dresser's shop and the Easter Bunny's egg factory have in common?

Both know how to do dye jobs.

What do you call the happy Easter Bunny?

A hop-timist Easter bunny.

What do you get when you mix a peanut and an Easter egg?

You get peanut butter eggs!

What do Easter bunnies love to do at the gym?

They love to egg-xercise!

What is the Easter Bunny's favorite Chinese dish?

It is hop suey.

What do you get when you combine the Easter bunny and a banana?

An Easter bun-ana!

What happened to the Easter egg under pressure?

It cracked. The pressure was too much.

What do you call those wild schemes the Easter Bunny comes up with?

Hair-brained ideas.

Why did the Easter egg teenager get told off?

He couldn't eggs-plain his way out of trouble.

What happens when you mix an Easter egg and dynamite?

An egg-plosion!

What does the Easter Bunny wear on her head?

An Easter bunnet!

What seasoning does the Easter Bunny like best?

Spring thyme.

What did the Easter Bunny ask the carrot?

"Can I have a bite to eat?"

Why was the adventure seeker thrilled Easter had come?

It was an eggs hiding (exciting) opportunity.

What is the competition between the cranberry-colored plastic Easter grass and the green-colored plastic Easter grass called?

A turf war.

What does the Easter bunny say before he eats his Easter eggs?

"Lettuce pray."

How did Momma Bunny teach the Easter Bunny to walk upright holding a basket?

One step at a time.

Why is the Easter Bunny's best friend a duck?

He always quacks the Easter Bunny up.

What did the egg put on his scratch?

A band-egg.

What is the Easter Bunny's favorite mood?

He loves being hoppy!

What does the Easter Bunny constantly overlook?

Its nose.

How close was the Easter Bunny to getting seen by someone when delivering eggs last year?

He came within a whisker of getting spotted.

Why couldn't the Easter Bunny take a flight to his favorite vacation spots?

He didn't have the hare-fare.

How can you tell how old the Easter Bunny is?

Just look for his grey hare.

What is the Easter Bunny's favorite story?

Any cotton tale!

How rich is the Easter Bunny?

He was a million-hare!

What does the Easter egg call a pot of boiling water?

A jacuzzi.

What do you call the Easter parade full of cats?

An Easter Purr-ade!

What do you call a purple Easter Bunny?

Easter Barney!

Why did the Easter Bunny wear two jackets in his painting facility?

The directions on the paint said to put on two coats.

Why should you never hide an Easter egg on a hill?

Because it will roll away.

What does a beautiful sunrise have in common with opening an egg for breakfast?

Both are the crack of dawn.

Why does the rabbit's nose twitch in the middle of its face?

Because it's the scenter.

Where does the Easter Bunny go for a haircut?

He goes to the hare dresser.

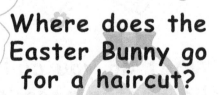

Who helped the Easter Bunny paint all his eggs?

Santa's elves who needed work when it was not Christmas.

Why couldn't the chocolate Easter bunny hear well?

One of his ears was bitten off.

In the Easter Bunny's lab, what's green and smells like yellow dye?

Green dye.

What do wanting to lose weight and uncolored Easter eggs have in common?

You have to dye it (diet).

What is the Easter egg's favorite pastime?

Telling yolks! (Jokes get it)

What's the difference between the Easter Bunny and a cornfield?

The Easter Bunny has two ears that hear great; the cornfield has hundreds of ears but can't hear at all.

Will standing in the sunlight outside on a spring day make you smart?

If you are fair skinned, it will make you well red.

How is the Easter egg's vision?

It is egg-cellent.

What is better? Chocolate bunnies or chocolate chickens?

Both.

Why was the river jealous?

Everybody was talking about the spring.

What kind of bugs pester flute players in the Easter parade?

Flute flies.

Can the Easter Bunny hop higher than the Eiffel Tower?

Absolutely! The Eiffel Tower can't hop.

What did the cheerleader say when asked to name the Egyptian sun god?

"Who? Ra!"

Why is springtime the Easter Egg's favorite season?

He fries too much in the summertime.

I thought the Easter Bunny and Easter eggs were the main focus of Easter and the sun, flowers, and bonnets were secondary, but guess what I learned in science class?

The sun is a star.

Why did the parade director ask for an Easter egg, root-beer and vanilla ice cream?

He wanted to make an Easter egg float.

What do you call Easter eggs that go to college?

Egg-ucated.

Have you seen the new camouflage Easter bonnet?

Me neither; it's top quality.

Why did the comedian put Easter eggs on him?

He wanted the yolk to be on him!

Where do Easter eggs like to sit on an airplane?

By the emergency egg-xit!

Why did the twin siblings sleep with Easter baskets under their pillows?

They wanted to have sweet dreams.

What happened when a fight broke out amongst the Easter candies?

The candies that lost got licked.

Why did the Easter Bunny go to the barber shop when his children got rowdy?

His wife said that he had a lot of unruly little hairs.

What did the scarf say to the Easter bonnet?

"You go on ahead; I'll just hang around."

Why did the Easter Bunny take the Easter egg to the playground?

He wanted to let it slide.

What kind of toilet does the richest Easter Bunny have?

A 24-carrot gold one.

How are bad jokes like Easter bonnets?

They go over people's heads.

What can be done to make the Easter Bunny nicer?

Replace the East with nice!

Why did the inventor place a small fan in her Easter bonnet?

She was trying to create a mind- blowing invention.

What's a wok?

Something a wabbit likes to hide behind.

Why was the girl even more pleased with her new socks than her Easter bonnet?

Easter bonnets will warm your head, but socks will warm your sole.

Why did the Easter egg cross the road?

He needed to get to the Shell station.

What grows on Easter egg trees?

Easter eggs!

Why didn't the female bunny want to leave her house?

Her hare kept sticking up.

How do you know if the Easter Bunny is an evil Easter Bunny?

If he leaves deviled eggs.

What was the Easter Bunny thinking as he looked at all of the tiny paper squares he planned to glue on the Easter egg?

"It's time to face the mosaic."

What did the Easter Bunny husband call his Easter Bunny wife?

She was some-bunny special to him.

Why did Mother Hen tell her egg not to roll?

She thought he was going to scramble.

What did the spring wind say to the boiling sun and the angry rain clouds?

"Hey, guys, I'm here to clear the air."

Who celebrates Lent year-round?

People who pick their belly buttons.

How do you keep Easter eggs cool?

You should put ice in the basket.

What's even better than an Easter float?

An Easter sundae!

Why does the Easter Bunny love to ride roller coasters?

It was hare-raising!

What is orange and peelable?

An orange Easter egg!

Why did the girl wear a yellow Easter bonnet and only a yellow Easter bonnet?

She was clothes minded.

How does the Easter Bunny make scrambled eggs?

With its whiskers.

Why do weathervanes make such great politicians?

They follow the wind wherever it blows.

Where does the Easter Bunny go to get a new tail?

He visits the re-tail store!

What does the Easter egg love to use in the bathtub?

His Easter, rubber ducky.

What is the Easter egg's favorite sport?

Bowling!

What is the Easter Bunny's favorite actor?

Rabbit Downey Jr.

What is the best way for an Easter egg to show its true colors?

It must come out of its shell.

Why does the Easter Bunny hide in the summertime?

He didn't have any hare conditioning in his house.

Why does the Easter Bunny love scary movies?

Because they are hare-raising!

How big is the carrot some kids put on the lawn to invite the Easter Bunny to hide the eggs?

It's a yard long.

Why is the Easter Bunny nice?

Have you ever met a mean rabbit?

What happens if the Easter Bunny sneaks back in your yard to reclaim some of his eggs?

It's a hare raid.

Does the Easter Bunny have amazing pens to color eggs?

Well, the ones that erase and re-write are certainly remarkable.

What happened when the spring wind touched the wind turbine?

The turbine took a turn for the better.

FUN FACTS FOR EASTER

Do you prefer milk or dark chocolate?

85% of people tend to prefer milk chocolate, with just 15% preferring dark chocolate.

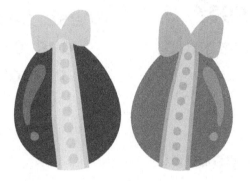

Do you know what favorite Easter treat would be ten times the height of Mount Everest if they were stacked on top of each other?

The 500 million Cadbury's Crème eggs that are created each year. 1.5 million of them are made in Birmingham, England every day.

CHAPTER 2

Knockin' On Easter's Door

"Easter spells out beauty, the rare beauty of new life." ~ **S.D. Gordon**

KNOCK! KNOCK!
Who's there?
Shirley.
Shirley who?
Shirley you must know that it is spring time outside!

KNOCK! KNOCK!
Who's there?
It is me, Annie bunny!
Annie bunny who?
Annie bunny you want me to be!

BRRiiNG! BRRiiNG!

May I ask who is calling, please?
Sure thing. It is Ann!
Um, Ann who?
Ann-other Easter Bunny. The last one got sick!

KNOCK-KNOCK.

Who's there?
Al R. Gees.
Al R. Gees who?
Al R. Gees make me sneeze, but I'm going to hunt eggs outside anyway.

KNOCK-KNOCK.

Who's there?

Art A. Ficial.

Art A. Ficial who?

Art A. Ficial (artificial) eggs often have candy inside them.

KNOCK-KNOCK.

Who's there?

Bach.

Bach who?

Bach about four generations, jellybeans were not given at Easter; the tradition only started around 1930.

KNOCK! KNOCK!

Who's there?

Heidi.

Heidi who?

Heidi eggs now quickly!

RING! RING!

Tell me who is speaking on the other line?

It is Chocolate Bunny Ear!

Um, er, um, Chocolate Bunny Ear who?

Can you repeat that? Someone just bit me!

KNOCK! KNOCK!

Who's there?

Izzie.

Izzie who?

Izzie time to paint the Easter eggs?

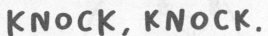

KNOCK, KNOCK.

Who's there?

Venice.

Venice who?

Venice the Easter egg hunt taking place? I can't wait!

KNOCK! KNOCK!

Who's there?

Boo!

Boo who?

No need to cry! It's Easter after all.

Buzz! Buzz!

Someone at the door?

Turnip!

Oh yeah? Turnip who?

Turnip the volume to start the Easter party!

KNOCK-KNOCK.

Who's there?

Rabbit.

Rabbit who?

Rabbit (wrap it) up with a bow.

KNOCK-KNOCK.

Who's there?

Bill Jerone.

Bill Jerone who?

Bill Jerone (build your own) Easter basket; you don't have to buy one at the store.

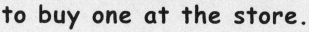

KNOCK-KNOCK.

Who's there?

Boyardees.

Boyardees who?

Boyardees Easter knock-knock jokes funny!

BEEP! BEEP!

Is there someone there?
Lettuce!
Lettuce who?
**Lettuce go now, we're late
for the Easter egg hunt!**

KNOCK-KNOCK.

Who's there?
Candy.
Candy who?
**Candy Easter Bunny bring
me a green egg this year?**

KNOCK-KNOCK.

Who's there?
Cher.
Cher who?
Cher your Easter candy
with me, and I will share
mine with you.

KNOCK-KNOCK.

Who's there?
Chalk a lot.
Chalk a lot who?
Chalk a lot (chocolate) candy
is always good at Easter . . .
and Valentine's . . . and
Halloween . . . and
Christmas . . .

KNOCK-KNOCK.

Who's there?

Dan D. Line.

Dan D. Line who?

Dan D. Line, daffodils, Easter lilies, tulips, and other spring flowers are in bloom.

KNOCK-KNOCK.

Who's there?

Midas.

Midas who?

Midas well be me or you that finds that special golden egg; somebody has got to find it.

BANG! BANG!

Who is there knocking at the door?

It is your friend, Bacon!

*Help me remember you please.
Bacon who?*

Bacon to go with your side of Easter eggs!

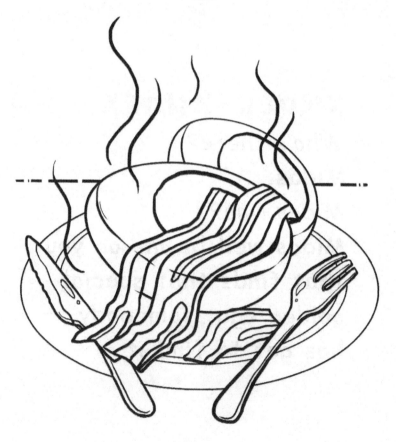

KNOCK-KNOCK.

Who's there?

Juana.

Juana who?

Juana come on an Easter egg hunt with me?

KNOCK-KNOCK.

Who's there?

Justin Casey.

Justin Casey who?

Justin Casey left a lot of eggs, I'm going to take a big Easter basket.

KNOCK-KNOCK.

Who's there?

Kahn.

Kahn who?

Khan you teach me how to dye Easter eggs?

KNOCK-KNOCK.

Who's there?

Ken E. Makit (can he make it)

Ken E. Makit who?

Ken E. Makit walking in just a raincoat through the cold rain, or will the Easter Bunny have to have an umbrella?

KNOCK-KNOCK.

Who's there?

Kerri.

Kerri who?

Kerri an Easter basket with you; I think the Easter Bunny has just hidden some eggs in our yard.

KNOCK-KNOCK.

Who's there?

Kenny.

Kenny who?

Kenny hide the eggs outside, or will the Easter Bunny have to hide the eggs inside this year because of rain?

KNOCK-KNOCK.

Who's there?

Poe Gogh.

Poe Gogh who?

Poe Gogh sticks are fun; we can hop like rabbits.

KNOCK-KNOCK.

Who's there?

Ray D. Aunt (radiant)

Ray D. Aunt who?

Ray D. Aunt (radiant) sunshine is expected for tomorrow's Easter egg hunt.

KNOCK-KNOCK.

Who's there?

Seymour Klearly.

Seymour Klearly who?

Seymour Klearly after the fog lifts; I believe the Easter Bunny hid eggs around here.

KNOCK-KNOCK.

Who's there?

Sir Cole.

Sir Cole who?

Sir Cole around the backyard one more time; we found eleven eggs and mom says the Easter Bunny probably left a dozen.

KNOCK! KNOCK!

Who is on the other side of the door?

You know me. It is Hoppy.

Hoppy who?

If you're hoppy and you know it, clap your hands!

BUZZ! BUZZ!

Who is there, please?
It is your neighbor Justin!
Are you sure? Justin who?
Justin time for Easter! Yes!

DING! DONG!

Who is there, please?
Hi there! Mya's my name!
Mya who?
**Mya Easter egg broke! Can
I get another one?**

BRRiiNG! BRRiiNG!

Howdy, who is there?
It is me, Arthur!
Really? Arthur who?
Arthur any more Easter eggs left?

KNOCK-KNOCK.

Who's there?
Tom Eight Toes.
Tom Eight Toes who?
Tom Eight Toes, tulips, Easter lilies, and other plants grow in the spring.

BuzZ! BuzZ!

Hello there. Who is at my door?

It is me, Finn!

I do not know a Finn. Who are you?

Finn-ish delivering your Easter eggs so you can rest!

KNOCK! KNOCK!

Who is there, please?

It is your cousin Harvey!

You sure? I do not have a cousin named Harvey. Harvey who?

Harvey great Easter everyone!

DING! DONG!

Who is on my back porch?
It is me, your friend Carrie!
Are you sure? Carrie who?
Carrie all your Easter eggs in one basket.

KNOCK-KNOCK.

Who's there?
Ty.
Ty who?
Ty a ribbon on your Easter basket so you can recognize that it is yours.

DING! DONG!

May I know who is there, please?

Kenya!

Kenya who?

Kenya save me some Easter eggs!

BUZZ! BUZZ!

Who wants to come in right now?

Esther, your favorite person at Easter!

Hmm, the name doesn't ring a bell. Esther who?

Esther-mate how much Easter candy you ate! Does your stomach hurt yet?

DiNG! DONG!
Who is ringing the doorbell?
You can't forget me. It is Hoppity!
Hoppity who?
Hippity Hoppity, there goes the Easter Bunny!

CHiRP! CHiRP!

Hello. Who is there?

Will!

Will who?

Will you find all the Easter eggs?

DiNG! DONG!

Who is ringing my doorbell?

You know me. It is Juan!

Juan who?

Juan Easter egg isn't enough. Can I have two?

KNOCK-KNOCK.

Who's there?
Ollie.
Ollie who?
Ollie kids are getting together after school for an egg hunt.

KNOCK-KNOCK.

Who's there?
Tom Sawyer.
Tom Sawyer who?
Tom Sawyer (Tom saw your) sister's Easter bonnet; he says she looks cute in it.

BRRiiNG! BRRiiNG!

May I ask who is calling, please?

Sure thing. It is Anoda!

Um, Anoda who?

Anoda Easter knock knock joke!

KNOCK! KNOCK!

Who is there, please?

It is your friend, Howard!

I do not recall knowing a Howard. Howard who?

Howard you wind up becoming the Easter Bunny?

FUN FACTS FOR EASTER

Do you know which flower is associated with Easter?

It's the white lily. It symbolizes new life and purity.

Do you know how big the tallest chocolate Easter egg was?

It was made in Italy in 2011, and was 10.39 meters, and weighed 7,200 kilograms. This makes the egg taller than a giraffe and heavier than an elephant!

CHAPTER 3

Easter Puns to
Make Things Egg-citing

"Where flowers bloom so does hope."
~ Lady Bird Johnson

Why was a little girl sad after the Easter race?

An Easter egg beat her.

Why do kids like to study their Easter baskets?

They want to know if the Easter egg or the Easter chicken came first?

How does a chicken lay all of those eggs without practicing?

She just wings it.

How did the Easter egg realize he was sick?

He had a medical egg-xam.

Why did the boy stick his nose outside on a gusty spring day?

He wanted the wind to blow his nose.

Why do Easter eggs like playing truth or dare?

They love to whisk it.

Why did the Easter egg smile a lot?

He was too egg-xited.

WOHOO!!!

Why do Easter eggs always like Easter?

They do not like dye-ing.

What spring toy is indecisive?

The kite is always up in the air.

Why do Easter eggs love eye exams?

They do not want to have scrambled vision.

What kind of idea was it to use eggshells to decorate during Lent?

An eggshell Lent idea.

How did the Easter egg climb the rock wall?

He scrambled to the top.

Why are there 13 eggs in an Easter egg basket?

The Easter Bunny likes giving egg-stras.

What is an Easter egg's favorite nursery rhyme?

It is Humpty Dumpty.

What do you call a robot bunny?

Hop-timus Prime.

What do the military and the spring wind have in common?

Both are known for drafts.

What do you call the smartest Easter egg in the Easter basket?

You call it eggs-traordinary.

How would you describe the Easter egg's home?

It is egg-stravagant.

Why did the Easter egg want to get out of its shell?

It was shell-shocked!

Where do Easter chicks find their jokes?

They use their yolk book.

Why did the Easter chick study karate?

He wanted to know how to crack Easter eggs.

Why did the Easter egg get a job promotion?

He did an egg-xellent job at work.

Why doesn't the Easter Bunny like having photos taken?

He can never get his hare right.

What do the Mardi Gras parade and a clothes dryer have in common?

Both have trappings of Lent.

What happens if you are amazed at how strong a spring wind is?

You may be blown away.

Why did the Easter egg teenager get in trouble with his parents?

He kept making egg-xuses about why he wasn't doing his chores.

What did the Easter rabbit say to the carrot stick?

I have loved gnawing you!

Why did the spring breeze go to the gym?

The gym had air conditioning.

How easy is it to learn to fly a kite?

It's a breeze.

Why should you never tell an Easter egg a joke?

Because it will crack up.

Why does the Easter Bunny love the springtime?

Love is in the hare!

Why did the spring storm finally calm down?

It ran out of wind.

What happened to the Easter bunny bully at school?

He was egg-spelled!

Why didn't the Easter Bunny win the pageant?

He had a hare that was out of place.

What did the police use to take the Easter chick to jail?

They used hen-cuffs.

Why did the baby bunny throw a tantrum?

He was hopping mad.

How does the Easter Bunny keep his hair looking so nice?

He uses his favorite hare brush.

What is the Easter Bunny's favorite exercise?

He loves Hare-robics!

What happened to the Easter bunny bully at school?

He was egg-spelled!

How are the people at the calendar factory planning to celebrate Easter

By taking a day off.

What did the Easter Bunny use to go around the world?

The Easter hare-plane.

What did the spring wind say to the stuck-up sun?

"Stop acting like the world revolves around you."

What branch of the military did the Easter Bunny join?

He joined the Hare force!

Why did the
Easter bunny keep
forgetting his
deliveries?

He was
hare-brained!

Why does the
Easter bunny drive
everywhere instead
of hopping?

Unfortunately, no
bunny knows.

What do you call
a rabbit that has
fleas that won't
go away?

Bugs Bunny!

April showers
bring May flowers;
what do May
flowers bring?
(No, not Pilgrims,
silly.)

June bugs.

Are Easter books
more fun to read
than regular
books?

Most are better
by a hare.

FUN FACTS FOR EASTER

Have you ever painted an egg at Easter time? Do you know the official name for egg painting?

It's called Pysanka, and it traditionally comes from the Ukraine, where they would use wax and dyes to color the eggs.

Do you know how long it used to take to make one marshmallow Peep in 1953?

27 hours! Nowadays each one takes just 6 minutes.

Did you enjoy the book?

If you did, we are ecstatic. If not, please write your complaint to us, and we will ensure we fix it.

If you're feeling generous, there is something important that you can help me with – tell other people that you enjoyed the book.

Ask a grown-up to write about it on Amazon. When they do, more people will find out about the book. It also lets Amazon know that we are making kids around the world laugh. Even a few words and ratings would go a long way.

If you have any ideas or jokes that you think are super funny, please let us know. We would love to hear from you. Our email address is - **riddleland@riddlelandforkids.com**

Riddleland Bonus Book

FUN RIDDLES
AND
silly jokes
— FOR —
KIDS AND FAMILY

50 bonus
riddles, jokes and funny stories

RIDDLELAND

SCAN ME

http://pixelfy.me/riddlelandbonus

Thank you for buying this book. We would like to share a special bonus as a token of appreciation. It is a collection of 50 original jokes, riddles, and two super funny stories!

Join our **Facebook Group**
at **Riddleland for Kids** to get
daily jokes and riddles.

Would you like your jokes and riddles to be featured in our next book?

We are having a contest to see who are the smartest or funniest boys and girls in the world! :
   1) Creative and Challenging Riddles
   2) Tickle Your Funny Bone Contest

Parents, please email us your child's "Original" Riddle or Joke and **he or she could win a Riddleland book and be featured in our next book.**

Here are the rules:
   1) It must be challenging for the riddles and funny for the jokes!
   2) It must be 100% original and not something from the Internet! It is easy to find out!
   3) You can submit both jokes and riddles as they are 2 separate contests.
   4) No help from the parents unless they are as funny as you.
   5) Winners will be announced via email or our Facebook group
      – Riddleland for kids
   6) Please also mention what book you purchased.
   7) Email us at Riddleland@riddlelandforkids.com

Other Fun Books for Kids!

Riddles Series

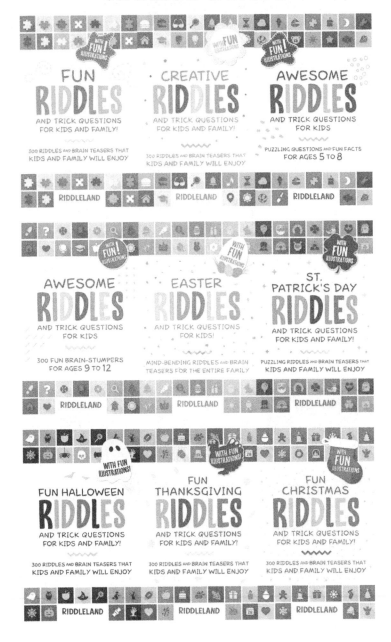

The Laugh Challenge Series

It's Laugh O'Clock Series

It's Laugh O'Clock
Would You Rather Series

Would You Rather Series

Get them on Amazon

or our website at www.riddlelandforkids.com

About Riddleland

Riddleland is a mom + dad run publishing company. We are passionate about creating fun and innovative books to help children develop their reading skills and fall in love with reading. If you have suggestions for us or want to work with us, shoot us an email at riddleland@riddlelandforkids.com

Our family's favorite quote:

"Creativity is an area in which younger people have a tremendous advantage since they have an endearing habit of always questioning past wisdom and authority."
~ Bill Hewlett

Made in the USA
Middletown, DE
28 March 2024